Political Messages
and Propaganda

Sean Connolly

A⁺

Smart Apple Media

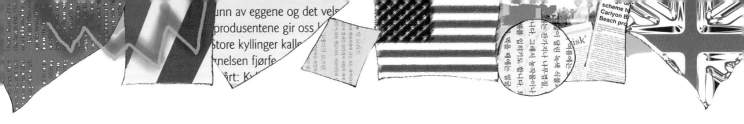

Smart Apple Media
P.O. Box 3263
Mankato, MN 56002

Printed in the United States of America

Library of Congress Cataloging-in-Publication Data

Connolly, Sean, 1956-
  Political messages and propaganda / by Sean Connolly.
      p. cm. -- (Getting the message)
  Includes bibliographical references and index.
  ISBN 978-1-59920-349-2 (hardcover)
  1. Communication in politics--Juvenile literature. 2. Propaganda--Juvenile literature.
I. Title.
  JA85.C683 2010
  320.01'4--dc22
                            2009003400

Designed by Helen James
Edited by Mary-Jane Wilkins
Picture research by Su Alexander

4720 9613 9/11

Photograph acknowledgements
page 6 Swim Ink 2, LLC/Corbis; 8 Vittoriano Rastelli/Corbis; 10 Dylan Martinez/
Reuters/Corbis; 12 & 14 AFP/Getty Images; 16 Hulton-Deutsch Collection/Corbis;
19 Alain Nogues/Corbis; 20 Richard T Nowitz/Corbis; 22 Designed by Propaganda.
Photo supplied by the Lancaster family; 24 Rex Features; 26 AFP/Getty Images;
28 Getty Images; 30 Lee Besford/Reuters/Corbis; 32 Corbis; 35 AFP/Getty Images;
36 Jacques Langevin/Corbis Sygma; 38 John Atashian/Corbis; 40 Ryuhei Shindo/
Getty Images
Front cover AFP/Getty Images

9 8 7 6 5 4 3 2 1

Contents

A Balanced Picture

"Loose lips sink ships." "Change you can believe in."
"Labour isn't working." "Because you're worth it."

These are some memorable quotes from the past 60 years. The first dates back to World War II, and seeks to warn people not to say too much about their jobs (in case enemy spies might use the information in the war). The next two are political slogans from the United States and Britain. The last is a phrase used in a series of television advertisements. Despite their differences, the messages share a goal—to change people's minds or to persuade them to do something.

Human Nature

One of the skills that sets humans apart from other animals is our ability to communicate at a high level. That skill runs through every aspect of human life, no matter where we live or in what sort of society. People communicate in a wide variety of different ways, ranging from the

A talkative American learns a lesson in this World War II propaganda poster.

prayers sung by a church choir, through the sales talk of a used-car salesman, or the words in a simple book that very young children study in preschool. Even monks who have taken a vow of silence can communicate with each other and with the outside world through their actions and the written word.

It follows that human beings can use these communication skills for specific purposes, which can often mean trying to persuade other people to do or believe something. Again, that is natural. Families discuss or argue about where to go on vacation. Religious people often try to convince others to follow their set of beliefs. Advertisers try to persuade people to buy a particular brand of car or breakfast cereal. Political candidates try to convince voters to choose them at the next election.

All these actions are common and everyday for most people. After receiving information about a political candidate, a breakfast cereal, or a set of religious beliefs, people can make informed decisions as long as they can find information from rival sources—for example, from other candidates or cereal-makers.

Taking Things Further

Things become different when individuals or groups distort information or prevent opposing viewpoints from being heard. Distorted information might include making false claims about a product or a viewpoint; alternatively, it might involve misreporting the views of rivals. This is the point at which persuasion becomes something very different—propaganda. At the most basic level, propaganda is a deliberate attempt to shape the way people think and how they behave.

People might easily understand and even support some types of propaganda —such as wartime efforts to shield painful truths from people. On the other hand, they might not even realize when they are hearing or reading propaganda. Everyone should be able to recognize this powerful tool, which can determine much in every part of our lives.

Rewriting History

People have been arguing, waging war, and trying to gain control over one another for as long as history has been recorded. Evidence from the time before written history —for example, paintings on the walls of caves—suggests that this was happening much earlier too.

An obvious way to defeat another group of people is to overcome them with force. But that is only part of the battle. Many experts believe that the victors also need to win over the hearts and minds of the other group. Doing this after defeating them might make them easier to control. Doing it successfully before a conflict can make a victory easier to achieve.

Trajan's Column is a 100-foot (30 m) high tower in Rome completed in 113 AD, celebrating Emperor Trajan's conquest of the Dacians (people who lived in south-eastern Europe). The column is covered in relief (carving) showing the victorious Roman soldiers.

Influence and Persuasion

Sending out persuasive messages aimed at winning people over or convincing them that it is pointless to resist is called propaganda. Leaders of the great civilizations of the past recognized its importance. The walls of ancient Egyptian temples and public buildings had pictures and other records of Egyptian victories. Defeated peoples were shown giving tribute to the all-conquering Egyptians. These messages helped Egyptians gain confidence; they also showed defeated people how pointless it would be to resist the Egyptian armies.

There is similar evidence of propaganda in other parts of the world. Huge stone carvings in western Asia tell of the victories of the Persian and Assyrian empires. They too show conquered peoples giving in to the greater force, and accepting that there is no point in rebelling. Ancient Chinese paintings showed the emperor as the center of the universe—another form of propaganda. Wall paintings in Mexico show how the Mayan, Aztec, and other civilizations held on to power by crushing opposition. Violent paintings show hearts being carved from captured warriors: a clear message for any adversary. The hearts were captured—literally—and the images remained in people's minds so no opposition was attempted.

What's In a Name?

During the seventeenth century there were some changes in the way people set about influencing others. To start with, the word "propaganda" was introduced. In 1622, the Catholic Church founded the Congregation for the Propagation of the Faith (*Congregatio de Propaganda Fide* in Latin). The goal of this department was to propagate (spread) the Catholic faith among the native people of the Americas and also within Europe, where many people had turned to Protestant faiths. Ideally, this would be done through persuasion and by setting a good example. However, religious disputes were often settled by force at that time.

Gradually the idea of propaganda—spreading a message rather than using violence—became more widespread. One major reason for this change was the development of the printing press. The first European printing presses began to operate in the fifteenth century, but it was not until the sixteenth and seventeenth centuries that printed materials became widely available. By the mid-1600s, Europeans were carrying out many battles—religious and political—on the pages of books and pamphlets rather than on the battlefield.

The eighteenth century saw the real blossoming of propaganda, as it entered the world of political thought. Great writers such as Voltaire and Rousseau in France, Burke and Paine in Britain, and Franklin and Jefferson in America fanned the flames of political debate. Hundreds of articles, booklets, pamphlets, and other publications tried to sway people's opinions about American independence, the French Revolution, the practice of slavery, and other important issues.

Former British Conservative Party leader Michael Howard campaigns in the 2005 general election. Politicians still use traditional campaign techniques, such as printed posters, balloons, and live appearances, although we are now in the age of the Internet.

GOVERNING THE GREEKS

Ancient writers often depicted defeated peoples as primitive or violent and not the equals of their conquerors. The Romans knew that they could not describe the Greeks (whom they ruled) in this way. But they still wanted to reassure themselves that they were somehow superior to the people who had developed many of the customs that the Romans followed.

The Roman poet Virgil found a way to praise the Greeks while noting how important it was for the Romans to govern them. In the *Aeneid*, he wrote: "Others [for example, the Greeks] shall hammer forth more delicately a breathing likeness out of bronze, coax living faces from the marble, plead causes with more skill, plot with their gauge the movements in the sky, and tell the rising of the constellations.

"But you, Roman, must remember that you have to guide the nations by your authority, for this is to be your skill, to graft tradition on to peace, to spare those who submit, but to crush those who resist."

Improvements to printing techniques also made it easier to print cartoons and other illustrations. Some works by William Hogarth and Thomas Rowlandson—often savage criticisms of life at the time—are as powerful now as in the eighteenth century. Political magazines were first published at about this time, developing the art of political cartooning and caricatures.

Into the Modern Era

Throughout history, people have used the newest technology—the latest media—to send out political and propaganda messages. Primitive cave art gave way to statues and wall paintings. Shouted slogans gave way to printed pamphlets, political magazines, and satirical cartoons. This trend has carried on into the twenty-first century, with radio, television, and the Internet becoming the latest media to be used for propaganda.

Sticks and Stones

Forceful messages can be easy to spot. Political messages are clearly identified during elections. Some propaganda is also obvious—and even expected—during times of war. But people can easily overlook the fact that political messages are pumped out all the time, although they might be harder to detect.

We are all exposed to indirect forms of propaganda in our everyday lives—articles criticizing a country that might soon become an enemy, one-sided radio call-in shows, or even biased learning materials used in schools. American academic Aaron Delwiche has summed up this contrast. "Propaganda," he writes, "can be as blatant as a swastika or as subtle as a joke."

Basic Methods

It's easy to become anxious about the quantity of propaganda that goes unnoticed around us. People sometimes decide that they will never be able to detect all that clever manipulation, especially if it is wrapped up in a slick media package. But with a little practice, people can learn to recognize some of the tricks that governments, companies, and other organizations use to change people's minds.

Opposite: North Korean soccer fans cheer on their team in a World Cup qualifying match against South Korea in March 2008. These young people live in a society where the government controls almost every aspect of daily life.

A short-lived propaganda watchdog provided some clear-headed methods of finding the persuasive messages hidden in the world around us. The Institute for Propaganda Analysis (see page 15) existed for only five years, but its influence is still being felt. And although new media such as television, cell phones, and the Internet have changed the way we communicate since 1942, many of the IPA's conclusions still stand. For example, the institute identified seven basic propaganda devices.

• Name-calling
• Glittering generalities
• Transfer
• Testimonial
• Plain folks
• Card stacking
• Bandwagon

People seeking to manipulate public opinion tend to use these techniques, or a combination of several of them.

Name-calling   People use negative words to describe rivals or opposing viewpoints: for example, calling someone else "mean with money" while describing themselves as being "careful with money."

Glittering generalities   This technique involves adding vague but positive-sounding words (such as "civilization," "love," or "freedom") to a message, so that listeners link the message with the words even if there is no obvious reason to use that particular word.

Transfer   Propagandists can "transfer" a respected group to support their message. An advertiser, for example, can suggest that scientists or doctors support its product by using a man in a white coat to sell it.

Testimonial   A testimonial is a famous person's support for something —which encourages others to support it. It is one thing for Tiger Woods to support a type of golf club, but is he really an expert on razor blades?

Plain Folks   This technique is especially popular in America, where politicians like to say that they are "just ordinary people" (who like junk food or chopping wood)—unlike the so-called experts they oppose.

Card stacking   This is one of the most extreme forms of persuasion —giving only one side of an argument. A newspaper, for example, might print only scientific evidence that supports its owner's opinion about global warming or other issues.

Bandwagon   People naturally want to be part of a wider group and draw strength from joining in. Propagandists sometimes aim their messages at particular groups (Christians, farmers, sports lovers) in order to tap into this.

Deciding on the best way to approach an audience is one thing, but even more important is choosing what the core message will be. Then it becomes easier to decide which approach —or combination of approaches—will be the most persuasive.

Sports legends Roger Federer, Thierry Henry, and Tiger Woods shave with Gillette razors as part of a multi-million dollar advertising promotion.

SPOTLIGHT ON
The Institute for Propaganda Analysis

The Institute for Propaganda Analysis (IPA) was founded in the United States in 1937. The world at that time faced threats from two powerful anti-democratic types of government: fascism and communism. Both these political systems used propaganda to gain supporters and to rule people within their borders.

IPA members believed that people in democracies needed to be alert and trained to detect propaganda. But their goal was to show how propaganda techniques could be used in non-political areas such as advertising. The IPA stopped operating in 1942 because it did not want to interfere with American and British efforts during World War II. However, the guidelines that it established for identifying propaganda are still relevant today, as is this quote from an IPA publication, The Fine Art of Propaganda:

"It is essential in a democratic society that young people and adults learn how to think, learn how to make up their minds. They must learn how to think independently, and they must learn how to think together. They must come to conclusions, but at the same time they must recognize the right of other men to come to opposite conclusions. So far as individuals are concerned, the art of democracy is the art of thinking and discussing independently together."

A FINE LINE?

Do you believe that it is possible or easy to identify propaganda when you come across it in daily life? Which tests would you use to distinguish between presenting a persuasive argument and distorting the truth with propaganda?

Over to YOU

War of Words

One of the most devastating examples of propaganda and its effects is comparatively recent in terms of world history. More than 70 million people died during the six years of World War II. Thousands more were wounded or became homeless because of the fighting. Many countries did not return to the standard of living they had enjoyed before the war for decades.

Germany's economy almost collapsed after World War I, leaving money practically worthless—just a toy for some children. Nazi leader Adolf Hitler used people's memory of those hard times for his propaganda during the 1930s.

A TERRIFYING CHILDHOOD

Owen Connor was a young child living in Liverpool during World War II. Sixty years after the war ended, he recalled how anti-German propaganda was as frightening as the bombs that fell on his neighborhood:

"To make people really hate the Germans the propaganda was at a high pitch. An example I remember was that they killed women and children, and bayoneted them, and even threw small babies on to fires. The slogan at the time was 'The only good German is a dead one.' It was quite common for adults to speak of such matters while we were in the same room. The adults assuming that being only five years old we would not understand. I was completely terrified, and with the bombing my nerves were shattered to such an extent I developed a very bad stammer."

Much of the responsibility for this tragedy can be traced to a single political leader, Adolf Hitler, and his Nazi party (which governed Germany just before and during that war). Hitler instilled fierce patriotism in the German people, urging them to share his views about Germany's need to gain control of Europe—and by extension, the world. In many ways, World War II can be seen as the story of a decent people (the Germans) who were tragically misled by propaganda. They—and the rest of the world—suffered as a result.

Finding Someone to Blame

Hitler believed that one of the main reasons Germany lost World War I was that it lost the propaganda war. He was determined not to repeat that mistake. From the time he came to power in 1933, he and his Nazi Party began to use propaganda regularly—and viciously. Much of this propaganda sought to make the German people feel angry about the way in which other countries (Britain, France, and the other World War I victors) had mistreated Germany.

Posters, films, speeches, and newspaper articles told how the "fatherland" (which is how Germans referred to their country) was mistreated by those countries. The other targets of propaganda were Jewish people within Germany and in Europe as a whole. The Nazis believed that Jews were constantly plotting to hurt Germany. By the end of the 1930s, after years of this propaganda, the Germans were ready to start another war and to attack the Jewish people in their own country.

Not Just History

People described World War I as "the war to end all wars" because everyone was so shocked by the death and destruction that it seemed impossible to imagine another such conflict. That statement proved false, and World War II led to millions more people losing their lives, health, or home. But even the terrible tragedies of two world wars have not stopped wars being waged: military experts have counted at least 170 wars since World War II ended in 1945.

With these wars have come new waves of propaganda. The U.S. military, for example, regularly overestimated the number of enemy soldiers that the Americans killed during the Vietnam War. Israel and its Arab opponents have accused each other of using propaganda for more than 60 years. The terrorist group al-Qaeda has mocked the United States repeatedly over the 9/11 attacks. Taliban forces in Afghanistan release boastful accounts of how strong they are, compared with the U.S., British, and other soldiers in their country.

Moving with the Times

Wartime propaganda has always stayed in step with the times, using the latest techniques to promote messages of fear, disruption . . . or maybe even hope in hopeless times. The Romans carved details on victory columns or along the sides of public buildings. Seventeenth-century Europeans used the printing press to spread their views. Much of the World War II propaganda was sent out through radios and newspapers.

Young North Koreans sit beneath an anti-American poster in the railway station of the country's capital, Pyongyang.

Nowadays, shrewd observers can find evidence of propaganda messages on television and the Internet. Both sides in conflicts now upload videos to file-sharing web sites. And new TV networks offer extremists the opportunity to promote their views through studio appearances and the videos they submit. Many weapons are now available to war propagandists.

Over to YOU

MAKING EXCEPTIONS

The Institute for Propaganda Analysis (see page 15) stopped operating in 1942 because its organizers did not want to disrupt the war effort. In effect, they were agreeing that some form of propaganda was necessary to defeat an enemy such as Hitler and his Nazis. Would you have done the same thing if you were in their position? Can you think of any times when you would turn a blind eye to propaganda?

Tools of the Trade

Every day we are bombarded with messages telling us to think again, make a new choice, or treat ourselves. If we followed the advice in all these messages, our lives would become a hectic swirl of new purchases and experiences. Maybe we would have fun. Maybe the rapid changes would be unsettling. One thing that is pretty certain is that we would run out of money fast.

Changing the way people think about an issue.

Presenting only one side of an argument.

Telling us that "everyone else is doing it," so we should too.

Letting us know that a film star or sport hero has made this choice.

These Moscow ads would have been unthinkable 20 years ago, when Russia's communist government banned private businesses.

SPOTLIGHT ON
Propaganda Advertising in Practice

A pale-skinned girl smiles at the camera against a black background as she holds a soft drink bottle to her lips. To her right, stark white letters spell out "Weirdo. Mosher. Freak. If only they'd stop at name calling." Below that heading, gothic letters spell out the name "Sophie."

The name—and the lettering—are clues. The photograph depicts Sophie Lancaster, the Lancashire teenager who was murdered in 2007 because she was a goth. Rather than seek revenge, Sophie's mother Sylvia has set up a charity in her daughter's name, literally. Sophie stands for Stamp Out Prejudice Hatred and Intolerance Everywhere. Sylvia turned to a Leeds-based advertising company called,

appropriately, Propaganda, to build awareness of the charity and its goals. She hopes to promote an understanding of how much different subcultures such as the goths' contribute to the richness of British society. Julian Kynaston of Propaganda understood the distance that Sylvia wanted to maintain between grabbing people's attention (in true propaganda style) and making the images too unpleasant:

"We could have easily used disturbing images of Sophie in the hospital that have been in the media to generate the shock factor, but Sylvia was rightly adamant that the campaign should be positive and peaceful." Instead, the images force people to stop, look, and think again.

If these phrases sound familiar, it is because they are the tools of propaganda. But even people who don't know what propaganda is would recognize them as advertising methods. So advertising can provide the first —and often lasting—experience of propaganda in many people's lives.

Business as War

The advertising industry uses many tools of propaganda every day. The difference between successful advertising and propaganda can be very small.

That is less surprising when we consider that an advertising agency and a military leader might be trying to do the same thing —persuade suspicious people that they are right.

The parallels go further. Agencies (large advertising companies) often spend months or even years developing a series of linked advertisements to promote a particular product. Grouped together, this series of advertisements is known as a campaign. Interestingly, a series of battles aimed at achieving a particular wartime goal (such as the surrender of an enemy army) is also known as a campaign.

Advertising campaigns help to build an image of a product, service, or organization. Like any propaganda, they seek to persuade people by guiding the way they look at things. If the campaigns succeed, people will have been won over even if they had noticed the persuasion and manipulation.

Sophie Lancaster (below) was beaten to death by other teenagers in 2007 just because she was a goth. A year later Sophie's mother set up the Sophie Lancaster Foundation in her honor with the goal of fighting intolerance.

WEIRDO. MOSHER. FREAK.

If only they'd stop at name calling.

Sophie

THE SOPHIE LANCASTER FOUNDAT
Stamp Out Prejudice, Hatred and Intolerance Everyu
www.sophielancasterfoundation.com

HARD-HITTING OR MISFIRING?

In 2002, American newspaper readers came across a startling advertisement showing a close-up of a teenager looking out from the page. Over her face was written (in letters small enough to make people really look hard):

"Last weekend, I washed my car, hung out with a few friends, and helped murder a family in Colombia. C'mon, it was a party."

Below the photograph was this explanation: "Drug money helps support terror. Buy drugs and you could be supporting it too." The text went on to give web and phone links for information about the drug trade. The advertisement, produced by the U.S. government, got a big reaction. TV commercials in the same campaign showed young actors playing drug users and saying casually that they tortured someone's dad or helped terrorists get fake passports.

Some people approved of these shocking messages. Others felt that using propaganda techniques (shock and playing on people's emotions) made the advertising somehow less effective—and wrong. Do you think that it is acceptable to use propaganda to promote such messages or is it misguided?

Over to YOU

Politics as Usual

Politicians in most democratic countries are often described as being "servants of the people." They achieve their position and power only by being elected by the people they serve. But the methods they use to win these elections—and to stay in power once elected—often stray into the world of propaganda.

All political messages, no matter what the system of government, address public opinion. Undemocratic governments control the media, so even news and entertainment can take on the role of propaganda. Huge posters urge people to work harder, hate foreign enemies of the government, and sometimes tell tales about neighbors who disagree with the government.

In 1997 newly-elected British prime minister Tony Blair actively encouraged the youth vote by inviting Noel Gallagher and other pop stars to his residence.

The political messages in free societies also seek to affect public opinion, but they do so with far more openness because voters turn away from governments that they believe are trying to mislead them. Nevertheless, major political parties produce campaigns that highlight their advantages and make no mention of their mistakes or failings. People expect a certain amount of this spin (see page 30) but too much can put people off. Sometimes, especially around election time, the messages become very negative: attack ads of the kind used in U.S. elections are often outright propaganda.

Going Right and Going Wrong

Politics in the television age depends on image, and political leaders (and their parties) try to make sure that their image is attractive and popular. For example, soon after he became Britain's prime minister in 1997, Tony Blair invited some of the country's young celebrities to 10 Downing Street (his London home). Television viewers saw images of Oasis songwriter Noel Gallagher, writer Nick Hornby, and comedian Ben Elton passing through a front door usually associated with world leaders.

Tony Blair and his political advisers recognized that these musicians represented a positive image of Britain that had developed around the world—a cutting-edge image of Cool Britannia. The prime minister knew that most of these musicians had supported his Labour Party in the election, and that they would be honored to be invited to Downing Street.

Trying to portray a popular image can sometimes backfire, though. In April 1992, a week before a British general election, the Labour Party organized a massive American-style rally in Sheffield. Party leader Neil Kinnock, who was ahead in national polls at the time, addressed the crowd as if he were a pop star. The plan failed because British voters considered the rally a stunt, and not in keeping with British traditions. Labour went on to be defeated in the election.

SPOTLIGHT ON
Political Party Commercials

It is illegal to broadcast political advertising on radio and television in the United Kingdom and the Republic of Ireland. However, major political parties are allowed five-minute slots to present messages to voters during the weeks leading to elections. This system allows the parties to put their message across but the controls mean that no party has an advantage. Other countries, including the United States, allow advertising as well as political party commercials, as the longer broadcasts give more of a chance to present a wider message.

Five years later, William Hague became leader of the Conservative party after a massive Labour general election victory. He set out to win the youth vote, notably appearing at a theme park wearing a baseball cap in the way he imagined a teenager might wear one. Like Kinnock's Sheffield rally, this idea also failed to win over British voters. Hague was mocked and he led the Conservatives to another defeat in 2001.

Barack Obama's election campaign developed local support across America, but at the same time was an effective fund-raising machine.

BUYING ELECTIONS?

People in democratic countries often worry about whether rich and powerful people can "buy" election wins. They point to the enormous amounts of money candidates raise—and spend—in their campaigns. The most extreme case is the United States. During the 2008 presidential campaign, Democrat Barack Obama raised $40–50 million every month.

That buys a great deal of newspaper advertising, as well as airtime on television and radio, so a candidate who raises less is at a disadvantage. That is why many Americans want to see an upper limit on the amount of money a single candidate can raise. The only real limit today is the amount an individual can donate to a candidate, which is set at $2,300.

The system in Britian works in a different way. The main political parties can spend up to about $27 million altogether in a general election. Individual candidates for Parliament also have a spending limit of between $14,000 and $19,000.

At the heart of these concerns is the future of democracy. Do you think that imposing spending limits also limits individual freedom (one of the cherished qualities of a democracy)? Or do you think being able to outspend your opponent gives you an unfair (and undemocratic) advantage in putting your message across to the voters?

Over to YOU

Spinning Yarns

Politicians have tried to influence voters since the Greeks developed the idea of democracy about 2,500 years ago. Despite the developments in communicating political messages to voters—such as newspapers, magazines, radio, television, and the Internet—much has remained the same. Political candidates still paint rosy pictures of themselves and their achievements while portraying their rivals as unreliable or reckless.

New Yorkers line up to protest against the U.S. invasion of Iraq during George W. Bush's visit to the city in June 2003. The signs of many protesters refer to the political spin that led the country into the unpopular war.

Since the 1980s, however, people have become aware of a new term to describe how political leaders try to influence the public—spin. The term was first used in the United States, where political journalists described the way that politicians try to manipulate news. The people who did the manipulation soon became known as spin doctors.

Different Spins

This manipulation can take many forms. One of the most extreme is the "non-denial denial." A politician (or someone representing the politician) responds to an accusation by saying "that is ridiculous" or "that is absurd." Despite the strength of these statements, neither actually says that the charge is untrue. In the same way, politicians can say that they never received money from someone trying to gain influence: in fact they might have received something else, such as jewelry or a free vacation.

Most often, spin doctors emphasize good news stories or government successes while playing down mistakes or bad news. For example, a spin doctor might announce that the government is planning to launch a new youth training program on the same day that thousands of people lose their jobs in the hope that the good news will take precedence over the bad.

Of course, spinning can backfire. Britain's Labour Party won landslide elections in 1997 and 2001 and had every reason to feel that it already represented British public opinion. But the Labour government took spin to new levels, led by prime minister Tony Blair's trusted aide Alastair Campbell (see Talking Heads, page 30). Journalists and the general public began to suspect that every bit of news had been spun by the government. And Campbell's reputation as a public relations wizard had declined by the time he left his post in 2003.

THE SPIN DOCTOR LOOKS BACK

For many British people, Alastair Campbell will always be remembered as the father of spin in UK politics. Campbell was a journalist who began working with Prime Minister Tony Blair in 1994. He used his media experience to help guide Labour to a general election victory in 1997. Blair then made Campbell his official spokesman.

That job involved making sure that journalists received and passed on news stories about the PM's activities. This in itself was not different from the job that others had held before him. However, Campbell used his media experience to ensure that news was interpreted in ways that would make the prime minister (and the Labour government) look good. People came to understand that Campbell used spin in every encounter with journalists.

About six months before Campbell resigned in 2003, he wrote about his earlier efforts to use spin to influence the news. By that time he recognized

how people had turned against that style of presentation: "The consequences were greater than we anticipated. We appeared, and perhaps we were, over-controlling, manipulative. People stopped trusting what we had to say. What we underestimated was the extent to which the changes we made in our relationships with the media and in getting our media act together would itself become an issue and a story. That's in part because we carried on for too long in government with some of the tactics of opposition."

GOTCHA POLITICS?

John McCain, the Republican party candidate in the 2008 U.S. presidential election, chose Sarah Palin to be his running mate. Ms. Palin was governor of Alaska, but was relatively unknown elsewhere. Her image as a pleasant next-door neighbor and loving mother proved immediately popular. Soon, however, she appeared to stumble and to be poorly informed about world affairs (essential knowledge for someone who could become vice-president). She gave confused answers to reporters' questions and seemed to make mistakes.

McCain and his party took the view that the publicity about Palin's supposed mistakes were examples of "gotcha" journalism. Just as people laugh and say "gotcha" when they have scored a point against someone, journalists seek to score cheap points by trying to get politicians to make or admit to mistakes. McCain even accused television journalist Katie Couric of "gotcha" tactics in an interview with Palin and him.

Do you think journalists are right to draw candidates into making statements that might be mocked later, or do you think they have a duty to expose ignorance and weaknesses in people hoping to be elected to powerful offices?

Targeting Children

People involved in producing propaganda find their jobs easier if they believe they have easy targets, that is, people who can be easily swayed. Some of the easiest targets are children. One of the main reasons young people are easily swayed is that they often think the best of people. In other words, children tend to be trusting and believe what they are told, especially if the words come from an adult.

This Nazi poster portrays the Nazi ideal of a blond young German student who carries the banner for his leader (Adolf Hitler) and the people.

Advertising, calls to patriotism, and even political messages are all aimed at children as well as adults. People are constantly trying to take advantage of the unquestioning attitude that children may have. Most countries have strict rules about how, when, and where advertisers target children, especially on television.

The In-Crowd

Propaganda often filters through to young people through their membership of organizations. Most people can be swayed by the bandwagon effect (see page 14), and children are particularly keen on being part of a larger group.

The Nazis knew the importance of this link between young people, organized groups, and propaganda. One of Germany's most noted organizations in the 1930s and early 1940s was the Hitler Youth. This organization was run like a club at local level, and many young people might have thought that it was mainly a social organization. But it soon became clear that the members were being fed information that would turn them into loyal Nazis when they became adults.

The Communist Party, which ruled the Soviet Union, had a similar plan, even though it was politically a sworn enemy of the Nazi Party and what it represented. Boys and girls across the Soviet Union were encouraged to join the Young Communist League branch in their city or town. These young people went on outings and to parties and sports competitions at which they absorbed the values of the Communist Party itself.

Playing Politics

Political messages can involve people who are too young to vote, or even to consider politics very seriously. For example, a famous 1964 television commercial for American presidential candidate Lyndon Johnson showed a young girl in a garden, picking petals off a daisy. She counts the petals, becoming confused and repeating the numbers.

SPOTLIGHT ON
One Man's Meat?

Parents are often concerned about what their children read. They might consider some books and stories disturbing, full of bad language, or unsuitable in other ways. Usually, though, they are unconcerned about heart-warming tales of loveable animals.

The novel *Saving Emily* is different. It is the story of a cow that faces an unpleasant life—and death—unless some local children can save her. Among those who reviewed the book was the vegetarian web site VegSource, which supported its message of protecting cattle from cruel treatment. The review highlighted how these cattle were "tagged, beaten, branded, hauled in cramped, filthy cattle trucks, sold at auction like a steak on the hoof, and sent to a feedlot for fattening."

This description was too much for the Center for Consumer Freedom, which considered it to be propaganda. Its reviewer argued that using such emotional language makes it hard for children to make up their own minds about whether it is right or wrong to eat meat.

The image of her face freezes and a man's voice replaces hers. He is also counting, but he is counting down in military fashion: ". . . Six. Five. Four. Three. Two. One . . ." Then the screen is filled with the image of a hydrogen bomb exploding. Johnson's voice comes on, urging voters to love one another. What the commercial does not say—but suggests —is that Johnson's opponent, Barry Goldwater, was an extremist who could easily lead the world into a deadly war.

More recently, people in the United Kingdom saw children being used to make political statements. By 1990, many people were worried about the disease BSE (or Mad Cow Disease), which was linked to eating beef. John Selwyn Gummer, the Minister for Agriculture, had the job of persuading people to continue eating British beef.

Although some scientists had doubts about BSE and its link to beef, Gummer encouraged his daughter Cordelia to eat a beefburger in front of the cameras. His message was clear: if he thought that there was any risk in eating beef, he would never have given his daughter the burger.

The birth of a polar bear in Nuremberg Zoo led German animal rights campaigners to protest against keeping wild animals in captivity. These protesters used child-friendly posters and costumes to attract attention to their message.

Born to be wild!

Würdet Ihr es seh'n aus meiner Sicht: Das Klima hier behagt mir **nicht!**

MENSCHEN FÜR TIERSRECHTE NÜRNBERG

Born to be wild!

Ich bin ein POLARBÄR - **holt mich hier raus!**

COULD IT HAPPEN HERE?

It is easy to say that Hitler Youth and the Young Communists belong to history and have no real link with today's world. But most political parties have youth groups, as do churches and other large organizations. Do any organizations that you know use propaganda to get a message across to young people? The College Democrats? The College Republicans? The Boy Scouts or Girl Scouts of America?

Over to YOU

Where Does It End?

In these early years of the twenty-first century, the world has entered what is called the information revolution. People can receive—and send—information much faster than at any time in the past. Every year there are new developments which bring us information even faster. The effect of this rapid change on propaganda is complex.

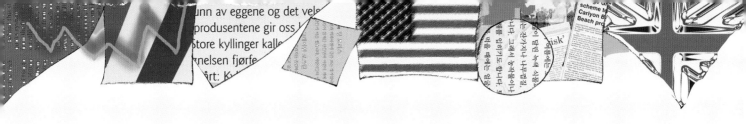

Reasons for Hope

On one hand, some people argue that new forms of instant communication provide people with more choice, which makes it harder to dominate the flow of information with a distorting message. These people point to the past, when everyone relied on just a few sources of information—word of mouth, town criers, and, later, printed material such as newspapers and pamphlets. A king or political ruler could arrest people who disagreed; publications that printed antigovernment messages could be closed down.

Even more modern media, such as radio and television, could be used to produce and spread propaganda. That is why, whenever rebel groups tried to overthrow governments during the twentieth century, they headed first for the broadcasting centers. News of the takeover—even if it had not fully succeeded—could be broadcast, and people would assume that a new government was in place.

That state of affairs held until the 1990s, when the information revolution really gained speed. Nowadays, the Internet and cell phone technology allow people to bypass official media and to send independent messages around the world. China is a case in point. As recently as the 1980s, the Chinese government had strict control over its people, helped by constant propaganda messages on radio and television. Optimists now observe that Chinese society has become more open—because, they say, the government cannot stifle the flow of information as it had in the past.

Opposite: Chinese university students led a protest in favor of more open, democratic government in 1989. Although the protests led to violence in which hundreds, and possibly thousands, of people were killed by government forces, China was later forced to introduce measures which made its society more open.

Or Maybe Not

Not everyone takes such a cheerful view of the information revolution. Pessimists note that instant communication can also mean the instant transmission of lies and distortions. Every child knows how fast a false rumor can spread through the playground, the school, and beyond.

Imagine someone being able to make up a hurtful lie about someone else and then being able to spread that lie around the world in just a few seconds. This is the sort of power instant communication gives people.

There is an old saying that "mud sticks," meaning that lies told about somebody are hard to remove from other people's opinion of that person. Pessimists argue that e-mails, blogs, and other Internet-related forms of communication help people spread propaganda instantly and at little cost. Worse still, individual supporters can spread lies on their behalf, while governments or political parties claim they are not responsible.

This behavior is antidemocratic as it offers little or no chance to deny the claims—however false or misguided they might be. Ultimately, the tools of communication are only as good—and as open—as the people who use them.

Comedian George Carlin (1937–2008) worked right to the end of his life, mocking the way governments, religions, and other large organizations limit people's freedoms.

SHOCKING CHANGES

The American comedian George Carlin (1937–2008) was a shrewd observer. He could see through spin and other subtle attempts to change people's way of looking at things. In the following routine, he showed how—war by war—military leaders had changed some familiar terms. The result was to make people less shocked by the terrible effect fighting had on ordinary soldiers:

"There's a condition in combat. Most people know about it. It's when a fighting person's nervous system has been stressed to its absolute peak and maximum. Can't take any more input. The nervous system has either snapped or is about to snap.

"In World War I, that condition was called shell shock. Simple, honest, direct language. Two syllables, shell shock. Almost sounds like the guns themselves . . .

"Then a whole generation went by, and World War II came along, and the very same combat condition was called battle fatigue. Four syllables now. Takes a little longer to say. Doesn't seem to hurt as much. Fatigue is a nicer word than shock. Shell shock! Battle fatigue.

"Then we had the war in Korea, 1950. Madison Avenue was riding high by that time, and the very same combat condition was called operational exhaustion. Hey, we're up to eight syllables now! And the humanity has been squeezed out of the phrase. It's totally shell shock now. Operational exhaustion. Sounds like something that might happen to your car.

"Then of course, came the war in Vietnam . . . and . . . I guess it's no surprise that the very same condition was called post-traumatic stress disorder. Still eight syllables, but we've added a hyphen! And the pain is completely buried under jargon. Post-traumatic stress disorder."

Rewriting the Future?

Politics and propaganda both have long track records and each is likely to continue long into the future. The question is: what sort of future will that be? Will it be determined by lies and distortion, or will people be better informed and so better able to make sensible choices?

Every year brings new challenges as well as new opportunities for people to benefit from the flow of information. Different media merge to combine quicker and more powerful ways of transmitting ideas. For example, people can send videos from their cell phones or use webcams to forge live link-ups.

In many parts of the world, young people keep in touch by cell phones. However, instant communication can also mean instant exposure to propaganda.

Few people in 1989 could have predicted how much would have changed by 2009. Are we in a better position to predict what life will be like in 2029?

Different Paths

The people who will be making their mark on the world of the future are the young people of today. They are growing up with far greater exposure to political messages, propaganda, and 24/7 information than their parents or grandparents had. That exposure could lead people in opposite directions.

Some might be swayed—back and forth and back again—by each new burst of information. Others might decide that enough is enough and turn their backs on anyone trying to persuade them to do anything. Neither of these approaches is helpful for society. People

THE CHANCE TO VOTE

On September 28, 2008, Austria became the first European country to grant 16-year-olds the right to vote in general elections. Young people in many countries, including the United Kingdom, have been campaigning for years to lower the voting age: in most countries, the minimum age is 18.

Twenty-year-old Scott Forbes is a British Youth Council volunteer who is part of the British campaign to lower the voting age. He recognizes that many young British people might be less excited at the prospect than he is. But speaking after the landmark move by Austria, he explained that British young people could be inspired to press for a similar change: "Although many young people in this country remain to be convinced about the point of voting, this is more a reflection of our democratic process than the ability of young people to express views and cast votes. In Austria they now have the choice."

who blow this way and that like weathervanes may grow up unable to think independently. Their future, and that of the society in which they live, will suffer as a result. Worse, this could open the door to persuasive people with bad intentions who try to manipulate public opinion.

The other extreme response, turning away from all sources of information, leads to apathy. People who can't be bothered to vote because the candidates all lie or because it doesn't change anything anyway are giving up the opportunity to promote change. Unfortunately many intelligent people—young and old—take this view and choose not to vote. They rarely think any further: do they really want to be ruled by a government chosen by other people?

Youth Involvement

Many young people are becoming more involved with politics, and this has some enormous benefits. It's good for people to become familiar with their government and the way in which it works as early as possible. The familiarity helps young people to make more informed choices when they become old enough to vote. Sensible, considered choices lead to sensible government, so everyone benefits. Informed voters are better able to understand political messages—deciding which are useful and which seem irrelevant.

Some young people, along with adult supporters, are trying to increase involvement even further by campaigning for a lower voting age (see Talking Heads, page 41). One leading British organization is the British Youth Council (BYC), which is led by young people for those aged 26 and under. The BYC helps young people become familiar with many of the concerns affecting them. It mounts campaigns to raise awareness of some of these—such as climate change and racial tolerance—while actively pressing for change in others. In 2008, the BYC celebrated its sixtieth birthday with its 16 at 60 campaign, aimed at reducing the voting age from 18 to 16.

COMPANY VOICES

In the future there are likely to be more links between governments and companies. Wealthy companies can help to fund schools (which are often short of money) or they may provide educational publications or web sites. They help young people learn the basics that could lead to specialized jobs in their companies. Both sides—the government (which funds schools) and the companies—are aware that the other side benefits from the arrangement.

But some people are concerned that the educational material produced by some companies is close to propaganda, and that children might not even notice this. For example, British politician Chris Huhne accuses ExxonMobil, a major oil company, of using propaganda on its educational web site (Energy chest). According to Huhne, the web site suggests that the cause of global warming is uncertain, despite overwhelming scientific evidence that burning oil products contributes to the problem.

Do you think that companies should become involved with education? Can teachers and students judge what is—or isn't—fair and objective?

Over to YOU

Glossary

24/7 Constantly, 24 hours a day 7 days a week.

9/11 The date September 11, 2001, when terrorists attacked New York City and Washington, D.C., killing nearly 3,000 people.

aide A trusted assistant to someone with great responsibility.

allies Countries that join forces during a war.

antidemocratic Opposing openness in society and the ability to protest.

Assyrian An empire centered in modern-day Iraq from about 900 to 600 BC.

BSE Bovine Spongiform Encephalopathy, a disease affecting the nervous system of cattle and sometimes called "mad cow disease"; some people believe it can be passed on to humans.

campaign A connected series of operations linked by a shared goal.

candidate A person who runs for a political office at an election.

communism A political system in which all property is owned by the community, and everyone contributes and receives according to their ability and needs. A Communist government provides work, health care, education, and housing, but may deny people certain freedoms.

democratic (of a government) Offering people the chance to vote for their leaders.

fascism A form of government that promotes military strength, a powerful central government, and a strong sense of patriotism—often linking it with a sense of superiority over other nations.

global warming The heating up of the Earth's surface, especially caused by pollution from burning fossil fuels.

Madison Avenue The New York street where many American advertising companies are based, and another name for the American advertising industry as a whole.

Nazi The name of the political party that ruled Germany from 1933 to 1945, which started World War II with its aggressive policies.

network A group of radio or television stations owned by a single company.

opposition (in a parliamentary system) The political party that opposes the government, and which is prepared to take over if it wins the next election.

Persian Describing an empire centered in modern-day Iran from about 550 to 330 BC.

propagation The spread of something, such as an idea.

public relations A public relations (PR) person or company acts as a link between a company or organization and the public, to explain the company's position.

running mate   A candidate for vice-president who stands for office as part of a two-candidate team (with the candidate for president).

satirical   Poking fun at something, such as problems in society.

Soviet Union   A communist country that included Russia and 14 other nations from 1917 to 1991.

subculture   A group of people who set themselves apart by the way they dress or speak, or by the music they prefer.

tribute   Goods or money paid to a conquering power.

Vietnam War   The war from 1954 to 1975 in which American armed forces tried—and eventually failed—to stop the North Vietnamese army from defeating South Vietnam.

World War I   The war from 1914 to 1918, centered in Europe between Germany, Austria, and their allies and the UK, France, Russia, and their allies.

World War II   The war which lasted from 1939 to 1945 in which Germany, Japan, Italy, and their allies fought the United States, the United Kingdom, China, and their allies.

vow of silence   A promise made by some monks not to speak to anyone so that they can concentrate on prayer.

Further Reading

1940s and 50s: The Power of Propaganda Steve Parker (Heinemann Library, 2002)

Political Manupulation: the World of Spin (Influence and Persuasion) Philip Steele (Heinemann Library, 2006)

Politics and Propaganda (In the News) A Hibbert (Franklin Watts, 2004)

Propaganda: Understanding the Power of Persuasion Spangenburg and Moser (Enslow, 2002)

Wartime Propaganda (Influence and Persuasion) Simon Adams (Heinemann Library, 2006)

Web Sites

American Rhetoric

http://www.americanrhetoric.com

Energy Chest

http://www.energychest.net/

Changing Minds

http://changingminds.org/index.htm

Project Vote

http://projectvote.org

Index